The cat and the mice

Story by Beverley Randell

Illustrations by Margaret Power

A big cat is looking down
at a little hole.

The mice
are inside the hole.

The cat sits by the hole.

The mice can see her.

The mice will stay inside the hole,
where they are safe.

The cat **stays** by the hole.

The mice are hungry.
They can not come out.

The cat goes to sleep.

Here come the little mice.
They are **very** hungry.

They see some bread by the can.

They run to get the bread.

The mice are eating the bread.

The cat wakes up
and she sees the mice.

The cat is coming.

The mice look up
and they see the cat.

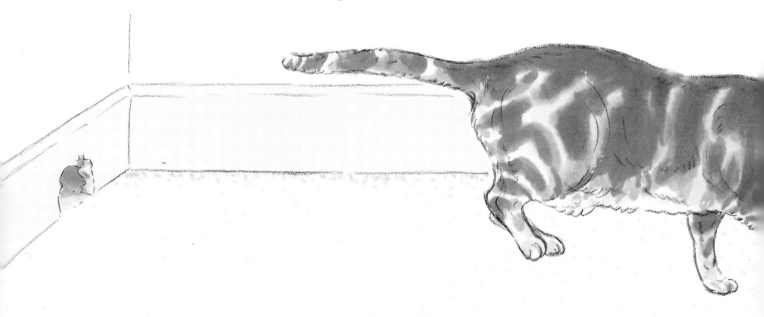

Help!

The mice run back
to the hole.

The cat is too old to run
after the mice!
They will get away.

The mice are back
in the hole again.
They are **safe**.